Grandpa's Rock Kit

by Donna Foley

illustrated by Burgandy Beam

Scott Foresman
is an imprint of

PEARSON

Glenview, Illinois • Boston, Massachusetts • Chandler, Arizona
Upper Saddle River, New Jersey

Photographs

Every effort has been made to secure permission and provide appropriate credit for photographic material. The publisher deeply regrets any omission and pledges to correct errors called to its attention in subsequent editions.

Unless otherwise acknowledged, all photographs are the property of Pearson Education, Inc.

Photo locators denoted as follows: Top (T), Center (C), Bottom (B), Left (L), Right (R), Background (Bkgd)

Cover ©Royalty-Free/Corbis; **5** (Inset) ©DK Images; **7** (C) Getty Images; **8** (BL) DK Images; **9** Tyler Boyes/Shutterstock; **10** (CL) U.S. Geological Survey; **11** Tyler Boyes/Shutterstock.

Illustrations Burgandy Beam

ISBN 13: 978-0-328-51404-5
ISBN 10:   0-328-51404-7

18   16

Every Saturday Danny and Tina helped their mother with chores around the house. One Saturday she had them climb into the attic.

Then Mom said, "Today we'll clean boxes out of here. It will be fun. Not every box is labeled. You never know what you'll find."

Danny found a big, heavy box.

"I think this box is heavy because it has some of Grandpa's rocks," Mom said as they unpacked the box.

"Grandpa collected rocks and stamps when he was your age," Mom said. "Later on, he made rock kits that customers bought. I bet we'll find a spare kit in this box. It looks like a board."

"Here it is," Danny said, lifting up the kit. "Grandpa must have known a lot about rocks."

A rock kit contains many different kinds of rocks.

"I'll share with you some of what Grandpa told me," Mom said. "Earth has three layers. The core is at Earth's center. The middle layer is called the mantle. The crust is the thin outer layer. It has three kinds of rocks."

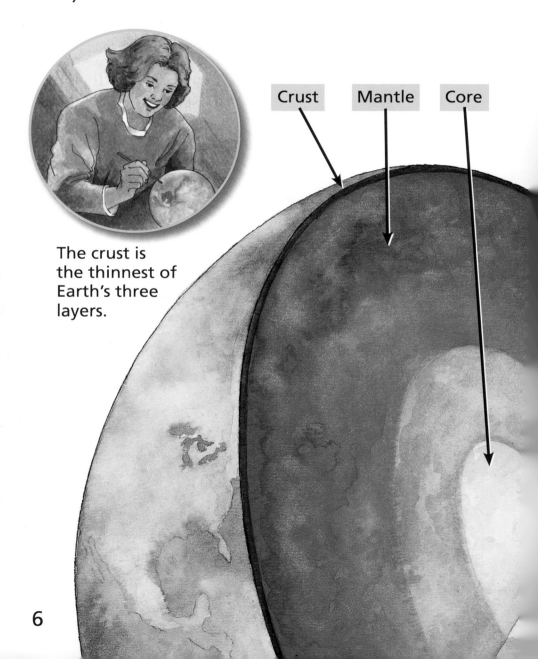

Crust   Mantle   Core

The crust is the thinnest of Earth's three layers.

"Igneous rock is the most common rock. It is made by heat. Magma is hot melted rock in the center of Earth. Sometimes magma pushes to the surface through a volcano. It flows out as lava. Cooled lava is igneous rock," Mom said.

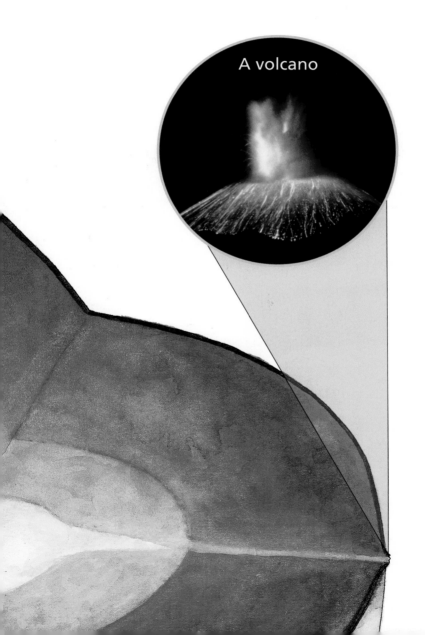

A volcano

"Granite is igneous rock. Granite is usually gray. It can have tiny white and black crystals. Some granite has pink crystals," Mom said as she held up a rock for Tina to see.

Granite

Igneous rock (granite)

"Another rock is sedimentary rock. Sandstone is sedimentary rock. Rivers carry sand to lakes and seas. Layers of sand settle to the bottom. The top layers of sand press down on the bottom layers. This pressing turns sand into sandstone. Sandstone is soft and sandy," Mom said.

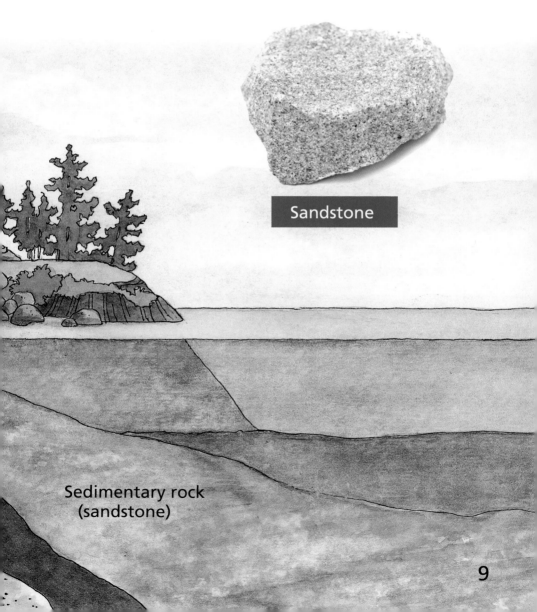

Sandstone

Sedimentary rock
(sandstone)

"Limestone is sedimentary rock too. It is made from sea animals' skeletons. Sometimes you can see the skeletons in the rock. Limestone is often white. It can be pink, tan, or other colors too."

Limestone with fossils

Sedimentary rock
(limestone)

Mom picked up another rock from the kit. "The third kind of rock is metamorphic rock. Heat and pressure change some rocks into metamorphic rocks. Marble is metamorphic. It has changed from limestone. Marble is usually white. It may have swirls of color in it."

Metamorphic rock (marble)

Marble

"Grandpa's rocks are really neat. Are there more?" Tina asked, looking at a piece of marble.

"Hmm," Mom said, "I think his entire collection is probably in one of these boxes. Why don't you guys try to find it?"

"That sounds great! Then you can tell us more about rocks!" Danny and Tina exclaimed.